# Flowers that Never Fade

*Flowers That Never Fade*

Illustrations by Judy Buswell
Illustration Copyright © 2000 Judy Buswell

Text Copyright ©1959,1990, 2000
The Brownlow Corporation
6309 Airport Freeway
Fort Worth, Texas 76117

ISBN:157051-5042

Cover & interior designed by Koechel Peterson & Associates, Minneapolis, MN.

Printed in the United States.

# A Special Gift

FOR

FROM

DATE

# Flowers that Never Fade

*Leroy Brownlow*

## Brownlow

# Contents

# Chapter One

# A Light for Living

*The Psalmist said, "Your word is a lamp unto my feet and a light for my path" (Psalm 119:105). The Bible is God's book of light. It sheds light on our origin, duty and destiny. It tells us from whence we come, how to live, and where we are going. It tells us how to live with ourselves, with our fellowmen, and with God. It is a foundation for our feet, a map for our eyes, a sword for our hands, food for our souls, and a healing balm for our hearts.*

The secrets of successful living are unfolded in its pages. The light in human books had its origin in the one great book, the Bible. It is the lamp from which all other lights receive their rays. There is a divinity about it that makes it shine among books like the diamond glistens among stones. It is the Heavenly Father's gracious

book of counsel and consolation to His children here on earth.

The undeveloped powers of the soul and the yearnings of the human heart demand a divine revelation which furnishes to us the help and strength of a Higher Power. If God exists—and He does—it is intelligent to assume that He would communicate with us, His needy offspring, in some definite and concrete manner—hence, the Bible.

• *The Bible claims to be God's inspired book which fills our needs.* It says, "All scripture is God-breathed and is useful for teaching, rebuking, correcting and training in righteous-ness" (II Timothy 3:16-17). It is God's book of science on right living.

The Bible has been criticized, tested, and weighed in the balance, but not a one of its truths has failed, nor one ray of its light grown dimmer. Nations have perished, customs have been altered, and manners have changed.

But age has failed to weaken its power. The enemies of the Bible perished and have soon been forgotten one after another, but the Bible keeps on living.

● *There is no other book comparable to the Bible.* It contains the choicest gems of thought, the wisest instruction, the highest code of morality, the sweetest comfort, coupled with a rareness and a richness unknown to any other book.

Christ's Sermon on the Mount is the greatest and sublimest code of morals to be found on this earth (Matthew 5:7). Is has been called the Magna Charta of Christ's Kingdom. There is in the sermon a beauty of words, a directness of thought, a brevity of instructions, and a simplicity of expression unlike any other message ever proclaimed.

Christ's Parable of the Prodigal Son is recognized as one of the classic stories in literature. It is regarded as the pearl of parables. It has been precious to all classes and ages people on every shore in every clime. It excels all human works of fiction in its portrayal of character. The tenderness of that father has helped millions to better understand and appreciate God's love for sinful man.

And what loveliness of devotion and true fidelity are found in the words of Ruth. Even Voltaire said the Book

of Ruth "was beyond anything found in Homer or in any other classic writers."

Words, verses, and volumes have been written on the romantic subject of love. But the Bible's definition of love outshines all human sayings on this heart-warming theme:

> *Love is patient, love is kind. It does not envy, it does not boast, it is not proud. It is not rude, it is not self-seeking, it is not easily angered, it keeps no records of wrongs. Love does not delight in evil but rejoices with the truth. It always protects, always trusts, always hopes, always perseveres. Love never fails.*
>
> I CORINTHIANS 13:4-8

This is only a sample and a small part of what is found in the Holy Bible. As we think and meditate together in the following pages, our thoughts will be

based upon the truths and principles of successful and happy living first given in the Bible. It is the key that unlocks our problems.

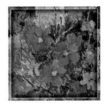

*The Bible is meant to be bread for our daily use, not just cake for special occasions.*

ANONYMOUS

# Chapter Two

## THIS TROUBLED WORLD

*No life is wholly exempt from suffering and distress. This has been true of man since the day Adam and Eve fell and were driven from the Garden of Eden. That was the day God said to man, "Cursed is the ground because of you; through painful toil you will eat of it all the days of your life" (Genesis 3:17). Not being able to look into the hearts of those around us, we think them fortunate and free from trouble, because we can only see the superficial signs of prosperity and success. But every heart knows its own suffering.*

• *Anxieties touch both the young and the old.* Trouble is no respecter of age. The young sometimes imagine that time will cure all of their problems, while the aged sometimes look at youth and think them trouble-free.

Problems vary with age, but every age has its own troubles and every heart knows its own care.

The perplexities of youth are so acute. They are faced with basic decisions that affect their entire future. They are so young and inexperienced to have to make such major decisions. Oftentimes their hearts break, and older ones do not understand. They have care enough to distress any heart and need the sympathetic help of those who have lived longer and have been over the road.

Those in middle-age also have their problems. They stand at the noon-day hour of life. They are passing from morning to the evening in life's little day. They must deal with career choices, marriage pressures and teenage children.

The older ones have their cares too. They have come a long way in the road of life, but they have never been able to get completely away from troubles.

• *Trouble comes to the rich and poor.* Wealth is no bar against troubles; often it serves only as a magnet which draws them. Trouble respects no one's person, fortune, or rank.

Disappointment and dismay, anguish and agony, sickness and death enter alike the homes of the rich and the poor, the exalted and the humble, the learned and the illiterate. In many a mansion there abides an ever-consuming sorrow hidden and unknown to the public. Fame, wealth, and other symbols of success often do little more than veil the sorrows of the heart.

• *Distress comes to the wicked.* They seek the pleasures of the world, but trouble always overtakes them. The fascinating allurements and the enticing amusements of sin increase our troubles rather than diminish them. The wise man Solomon laid down this principal of life: "Remember your Creator in the days of your youth,

before the days of trouble come and the years approach when you will say, "I find no pleasure in them" (Ecclesiastes 12:1). Sin is a thief that steals joy from a world that already has too little of it.

• *Disturbance also comes to the righteous.* The apostle Paul was one of the best men of all ages, but trouble followed him like a shadow. He suffered affliction and persecution more than many others of his day— he even died a martyr's death. But he learned to suffer gracefully and to profit from adverse experiences. He saw his sufferings as blessings in disguise. He wrote, "Now I want you to know, brothers, that what has happened to me has really served to advance the gospel" (Philippians 1:12). He found refuge in his distresses. He found the secret of dealing with life's un-pleasantries. Hence, he wrote, "I have learned to be content whatever the circumstances" (Philippians 4: 11). His attitude took the poison out of life's cruel bite.

There is no mistake about it—this earth is not heaven. The pathway of life is crowded with sorrows. But every traveler may so walk as to enter the land where sorrows are unknown.

*The path of sorrows and*
*that path alone*
*Leads to the land where*
*sorrow is unknown.*
*No traveler ever reached*
*this blest abode*
*Who found not thorns and*
*briers in his road.*

WILLIAM COWPER

©1994
Lindy Pesciett

# Chapter Three

# STRENGTH IN
# TIMES OF
# SUFFERING

*There are many kinds of suffering—physical pain, mental anxiety, bereavement, and a world of others. But regardless of the kind, our calamity is God's opportunity.*

• *Belief in God as a refuge and a present help always strengthens us.* Faith in God turns our dark clouds to sunshine, because we believe this precious truth: "And my God will meet all your needs according to his glorious riches in Christ Jesus" (Philippians 4:19). Needs! Needs! A thousand needs! And God shall supply all of them. Supply not what we may want, but what we need.

*Before me, even as behind,*

*God is—and all is well.*

JOHN GREENLEAF WHITTIER

Faith in God strengthened the writer of Psalms when he was almost at the fainting point. He said, "I am still confident of this: I will see the goodness of the Lord in the land of the living" (Psalm 27:13). He had experienced a close call. But at the height of the crisis, faith lifted him up and gave him strength. If we draw nigh to God, He will draw nigh to us, and any person close to God is never alone and never far from help.

*Though destruction walk around us,*

*Though the arrow past us fly,*
*Angel-guards from Thee surround us;*
*We are safe if Thou art nigh.*

AUTHOR UNKNOWN

• *In our distress we find the capacity for endurance through prayer to God.* David said, "I call on the Lord in my distress, and he answers me" (Psalm 120:1). In the hour of ease we may think we can get along without God. Of course, we cannot; we just think so. But in the hour of distress when all other help fails us, then up goes our cry to the Father, because there is no fear the Heavenly Father cannot quiet, and there is no heartache He cannot cure.

> *Sometimes God answers our prayers with a complete deliverance from distress, and sometimes with a modification of that agony, and at other times by granting blessings whereby we are able to bear it patiently. God does not always answer our prayers by giving us exactly what we ask. He loves us too much for this. Instead, He gives us what is best for us.*

> *The Lord will either calm your storm, or allow it to rage while He calms you.*
>
> ANONYMOUS

Admist all dangers, afflictions, and embarrassments, many have experienced through prayer the calmness, tranquillity, and sweetness of life promised in this passage: "Do not be anxious about anything, but in everything, by prayer and petition, with thanksgiving, present your requests to God. And the peace of God, which transcends all understanding, will guard your hearts and your minds in Christ Jesus" (Philippians 4:6-7).

• *God's gracious providence affords courage to all who love the Lord.* The Bible says, "And we know that in all things God works for the good of those who love him, who have been called according to his purpose" (Romans

8:28). The adversities of life will be overruled by the almighty and wise God to produce the eternal and permanent good of those who love the Lord. This promise gives us strength for every eventuality.

Trials and afflictions teach us the truth about our transitory condition, and take our affections from this world and center them on things eternal. They produce a subdued patience, a humble temper, and a kind disposition. However, adversities often have the opposite effect on some. They are hardened by their refusal to submit to the obvious design of suffering. But the Christian in his suffering, like Job of old, sins not nor charges God foolishly (Job 1:22). He understands the chastisement is for his good (Hebrews 12:5-11).

Even though adversities and trials have never seemed good at the time, all saints have seen their value and toward the end of life have said that it was good for them to have been afflicted. David said, "Before I was afflicted I went astray, but now I obey Your word. It was good for me to be afflicted so that I might learn Your decrees" (Psalm 119:67-71).

Out of our human weaknesses, there may come moments when we are tempted to doubt that all things are working for our good. This is due to our shortsightedness. We are tempted to think in the limited terms of the present and to appraise in the narrow scope of what we presently feel and see. Though our trials and afflictions are numerous and long-endured, we know from God's revelation and from our own experiences that they work for our good—that is, if we love God. For this is a conditional promise— "to love them that love God."

• *We may obtain rest form our burdens simply by casting them on the Lord.*

David said, "Cast your cares on the Lord and He will sustain you" (Psalm 55:22). And Peter said, "Cast all your anxiety on him because he cares for you" (I Peter 5:7). The weight of life's cares and sufferings are too burdensome for us to try to carry them alone. We should cast them on the Lord and take a rest.

Jesus says, "Come to me, all you who are weary and burdened, and I will give you rest" (Matthew 11:28). Rest is a necessity in our being and in the nature of all things. The ground, vegetation, animals, and machinery need rest. Our body also demands rest. All human organs need rest. Because of this need, God has provided rest for us. He divided the time between day and night, and separated the year into planting, plowing, reaping, and respite. Even Christ had to withdraw from the multitudes to allow His body to rest. Nature, reason, and the Scriptures all teach God's law of rest.

• *We may think ourselves to victory over suffering.* Or we may think ourselves to defeat. Solomon said as a man "thinketh in his heart, so is he" (Proverbs 23:7 KJV). No one is ever stronger than his thoughts. Both cowards and heroes are the results of their thinking.

"Stone walls do not a prison make, nor iron bars a cage." The world is filled with people who have become prisoners of their own thinking. Their own attitudes have imprisoned them. Prison bars of iron are hard and unyielding, but a thought is a stronger bar than one made of iron. One of the characters created by Charles Dickens was right when he said, "I wear the chains I forged in life." Indeed, we bind ourselves by the chains we forge. If we have become captives to our own thoughts of despair and defeat, we can never find freedom and relief until we change our thinking.

Self-pitiers are usually self-defeated persons. They usually imagine they have the most difficulties, the hardest time, and the maximum of grief. Their longing for sympathy only deepens their gloom and defeat.

We need to say in the language of Paul, "I can do everything through Him that gives me strength" (Philippians 4:13). There is power in saying "I can." "I can't" has defeated many a person. Success comes in "cans"; failures come in "can'ts."

We have strength —physical, moral, and mental—that we have never dreamed of. When the occasion calls for it, we can draw from that dormant strength through the power of victorious thinking. Whatever the problem is, say, "With God, I can solve it." Whatever the sorrow is, say, "With God, I can bear it." Whatever the suffering is, say, "With God, I can endure it." Say, "I can; I can;

I can." Say it again and again and let God begin his work.

● *Gratitude for the blessings we have relieves the sting from the afflictions we must often suffer.* Gratitude to God not only honors Him, but blesses us. It is always refreshing to recall, "Every good gift and perfect gift is from above, coming down from the Father" (James 1:17). May we never forget it.

No matter how heavy and low the clouds hang, the sun is shining somewhere. The Godward side of every cloud is always bright. Our afflictions may be numerous, but so are our blessings. Our sorrows may be heartbreaking, but our joys can be heart-healing. We have never seen circumstances so bad, but what they could be worse.

Some people, however, destroy themselves through their own ingratitude. Ungratefulness robs us of one of the noblest qualities.

Many people are miserable because they are unthankful. Any trait we cultivate will grow. As selfishness increases so does ingratitude. One feeds the other and both grow.

The ungrateful mind is always a discontented mind. It fails to recognize God's many blessings. The ungrateful person cannot enjoy the blessings he has for fretting over the blessings he does not have. The secret of gratitude is in making the most of what we have. The secret of contentment is in making the least of what we lack. A deep gratitude for what we have will take the fret out of what we lack. The battle is half won by counting our blessings. Count them. You will be surprised.

# Chapter Four

# PEARLS OF LIFE

*There* are many blessings to be derived form sufferings, if we accept them analytically and gracefully. Otherwise, there is the danger of frustration and rebellion. The cynic is invariably a person whose hopes have been thwarted. It is our reactions to our troubles that either help or harm us.

If we are made of the right stuff, distress can help us to discover the pearls of life.

> The burden of suffering seems
> a tombstone hung about our
> necks, while in reality it is
> only the weight which is
> necessary to keep down the
> diver while he is hunting
> for pearls.
>
> RICHTER

• *Through sickness people may become better acquainted with themselves.* Modern life is lived at high speed. There is so much hurry and rush over things that are relatively unimportant. Life's competition has never before been so keen and strenuous. Consequently, many of us are pushing ourselves to the breaking point—nervous indigestion, stomach ulcers, tattered nerves, and sleepless nights. The cares of the world are written all over our faces. Little time for prayer, Bible reading, and deep meditation which feeds the soul! The mad rush of a chaotic civilization has estranged some from their deeper self. They have become strangers to themselves.

Then sickness comes. The wheels of a busy routine are slowed down. This enforced idleness compels them to think, think, and think. Through thinking they become acquainted with themselves all over again. They come to know the real meaning of life. They learn their true self and what their real needs are—that they have longings for peace of heart which can never be satisfied with the material things of life.

They have learned the hard way, but they have learned! So if a fevered and restless brow has helped to cool and calm a fevered and restless soul, then the suffering has not been in vain. If sickness has led one to know oneself, then it has truly had its compensation.

• *Distress may help us to better know the Lord.* Through our veil of tears, we see in a new light Him who was "despised and rejected by men, a man of sorrows, and familiar with suffering" (Isaiah 53:3). We become better acquainted with Christ when we experience His teaching, love, and sympathy in times of suffering and sorrow. In suffering Jesus becomes a necessity to us—not just a half hearted luxury. We come to know Him better, because we need Him more. Through pain we feel a more appreciative touch of His hand. Through the agony of our afflictions we hear a new tenderness in His voice. Through the recognition of our own helplessness we feel a new strength in His strong arms about us.

A blind man once said, "I never did see until I became blind." Not until this affliction came upon him was he

able to get his eyes of discernment open. Not until he became blind to one world was he able to see another. When his material eyes were closed, his spiritual eyes were opened. Then for the first time he was able to see the invisible.

Suffering has the power to teach us our inadequacy. It shows us that we have trusted in our weak humanity too long. It proves to us that we need help we cannot muster and power that we cannot generate. Our distress may encourage us to trust in the Lord, for it shows the folly of trusting in self. If it has that effect, then the sufferer has been rewarded.

*Trust in the Lord with all your heart and lean not on your own understanding.*

PROVERBS 3:5

• *Sickness may be the means of cultivating friendships.* Kind and loving friends come to our assistance and help us carry our burdens. Never before did a kind word, a warm hug, and sympathetic prayer mean so much. Friendships take on a greater value.

These words have often come from the lips of the sick, "I never knew I had so many friends." Well, they had been standing by all of the time. Maybe the sick person had allowed those friendships to get in bad repair—not intentionally but through neglect. Now he vows that when he gets well he is going to be a better friend, that he is going to visit more, send more cards, and do more to help others. Good vows! Those who have been awakened to make them should keep them.

If illness leads us to repair friendships, then this unhappy experience has had another reward.

1993
Judy Buswell Marshall

*A man that has friends must be friendly.*

PROVERBS 18:24

• *Suffering allows us to be used as God's comforters.* We cannot fully understand the other person's problems until we have experienced similar ones. We shall never know how heavy another's burdens are until those weights have rested on our own shoulders. Distress may add tenderness to our hearts and nobility to our lives. It can bring us closer together. And as John Henry Newman said, God does not comfort us to make us comfortable, but to make us comforters.

# Chapter Five

# CHEERFUL HEARTS

*As a small boy was eating his dinner, the sparkling, golden rays of the setting sun fell upon his spoon. He put the spoon to his mouth and playfully exclaimed in his childish make-believe, "Mama, I have swallowed a spoonful of sunshine." How excellent it would be if many of us grown-ups could swallow a few spoonfuls of sunshine. It would do some of us more good than medicine. The wise man Solomon had this in mind when he said, "A cheerful heart is good medicine, but a crushed spirit dries up the bones" (Proverbs 17:22). Cheerfulness contributes to sanity and good health. It doubles the value of food and sleep, lightens the burden of every care, and gives the heart courage to face every problem.*

There is dismay sometimes for which we are not responsible. Circumstances place us amid conditions which are most disheartening. Sometimes this cannot be avoided. But the vast majority of gloomy people simply "achieve" dismay. They have made themselves wretched; they have brought it upon themselves; and they alone are to blame for being miserable.

It is natural that unhappy people ask the cause of this dismay. David did. He sought an explanation of his depression by asking, "Why are you downcast, O my soul? Why so disturbed within me?" (Psalm 42:5). Why? Yes, why are we sorrowful?

• *One thing that causes low spirits is sin.* Remorse gnaws at the heart. Conscience can make wretches of us all. And there is no satisfying relief until we experience the healing cure of forgiveness. When forgiven, then we should put it behind us.

There was enough sin in the apostle Paul's past to forever make him miserable—that is, if he had brooded over it. But by the grace of God he received forgiveness, and put it behind him, forgot it, and reached forth to the things before him (Philippians 3:13,14). This is the only happy to way to live. One great reason for rejoicing is forgiveness.

• *Another everyday cause of dismay with some people is conceit.* In this case, gloom is the product of an exaggerated egotism.

Some people enjoy being the "whole show." But if someone even hints that they are not as brilliant or important as they think they are, they become most miserable. The conceit of many has robbed them of much sunshine. Their state is aptly described by what Canovas said of Costello, the Spanish politician. He said that Costello was so anxious for notice and high position he could not enjoy a wedding, because, not being the bridegroom, he could not receive the most attention and that he could not appreciate a funeral, because he was not he corpse about whom most of the people were thinking.

God's remedy for this trouble is found in the Bible: "For by the grace given me I say to every one of you: Do not think yourself more highly than you ought" (Romans 12:3).

• *Another cause of mental depression is an exaggerated inferiority complex.* We say "exaggerated," because perhaps every person has an inferiority complex. The difference is that some exaggerate it. Yes, some may appear to have a superiority complex and take on the brass and bluster of a superman, but perhaps beneath the surface there is that deep and common feeling of inferiority. But inferiority can be adjusted to the honor and achievement of a person.

Admittedly, there are diversities of gifts. "These members do not all have the same function" (Romans 12:4,5). Thus we may need to change goals in life. If we cannot be an Abraham Lincoln or a Babe Ruth, we can be a useful and honored salesperson, physician, carpenter, farmer, nurse, seamstress, or homemaker.

It is the law of nature that ability and talent can increase. The weakness of one arm may lead to strength in the other. Blindness has its compensation in the development of keener senses of touch and hearing. One weak lung is offset by the increased strength of the other. What is true of us physically can also be true of us emotionally. The possibilities of superiority through compensation for inferiority is illustrated in some of the best know lives in history. The biographies of Aristotle, Wagner, Stevenson, Pope, Bacon, Parkman, and Keats indicate that their lives were shaped by their disabilities.

Man alone has the feeling of inferiority, and man alone attempts to compensate for it. It can be the spark in your life to ignite a power that you did not know you had.

• *Another reason for gloom with many people is the folly of borrowing trouble.* "It is ills that never happened that have mostly made men miserable," says Tupper. Never borrow trouble. The calamity you dread may never come. If it should come, it is folly to pay interest on it in advance. If it does come tomorrow, you will be better able to meet it by reserving today's strength.

Jesus taught us this lesson: "Each day has enough trouble of its own" (Matthew 6:34). This does not encourage laziness or irresponsibility. Instead, it teaches us to live life a day at a time. After all, this is the only

way it can be lived. Yesterday cannot be lived for it is gone. Tomorrow cannot be lived for it has not come. All that we have is today. And the best preparation we can make for the future is to take care of our duties today. Hold your imagination in check. This makes life cheerful.

● *Another thing that disturbs some of us is the harboring of malice.* There can be no inward peace when one is filled with hatred. We are smart if we free ourselves of that which would warp our personality and destroy us. Some return evil for evil at the dear price of destroying themselves. They get even by pulling themselves down to the level of their enemies.

It is no marvel that God has said, "Do not repay anyone evil for evil….It is mine to avenge; I will repay says the Lord" (Romans 12:17-19). This is for our welfare. And happy is the one who abides by it.

A man once went to President Lincoln and stated that he had been abused by a congressman and wanted his advice. Lincoln said, "Write out the account and bring it to me." This was done, and the president read the paper. Lincoln then said, "That is good; now take it home—keep it till tomorrow, read it, then burn it."

We are in the pursuit of happiness if we learn to forget the wrongs we suffer.

*Cheerfulness is the atmosphere in which all things thrive.*

JOHANN PAUL RICHTER

Chapter Six

MOTIVES TO CHEERFULNES

*No matter what happens, keep up your courage. Be brave. Bravery leads to victory, but cowardice leads to defeat. Shakespeare profoundly expressed it in these words:*

> *Cowards die many times before their death,*
> *The valiant never taste of death but once.*

Cowards die a thousand times before death really comes. Through their own temperament they assign themselves to the narrow and harassing confines of a living death. This kind of dying—death of faith, death of hope, death of cheer, death of personality—is worse than death of the body.

Life is sacred and time is precious, too precious to waste any of it by making

ourselves a kind of living corpse which does little more than breathe and stare. So let us live while we live, for death will come soon enough.

There are so many things to stimulate us to cheerfulness; for instance:

• *One motive to cheerfulness it that others have troubles as well as we*— not that we rejoice in others' adversities, but it does help us to understand that we are no different from others. A suffering world pictures to us the realities of life. It teaches us that life must be lived in the world of reality rather than spent in sheltered dream castles. Trouble is one thing to which all of us are heir. Your neighbor may not have your trouble, but he has his own, which may be worse than yours. Trouble is visited alike on the rich and the poor, the high and the lowly—there is no exception.

A king, riding in his splendid and costly chariot, passed a stone cutter

by the side of the road. As the man of toil looked up he said to himself, "Oh, if I could be like that man—no work, no problems, no worries." Just at that moment the king looked down and said to himself, "Oh, if I could have been born like that man—no problems, no cares; work is so much sweeter than worry." It is true that the king had no problem in paying his grocery bill and his house rent, but he had the worries of forty million people and the problem of retaining his crown.

When we learn to sing in the rain we have made real progress in the development of personality. We must bear troubles bravely and with a hopeful heart. If we wait until we have no troubles to be cheerful, then our days will never be blessed with cheer. Instead, our life will be a continuous nightmare of despondency, for there will be no dawning of troubleless days in this life. Remember—this earth is not heaven.

• *Another incentive producing cheerfulness is that it honors Christianity.* A gloomy, bitter, pessimistic person is not a good advertisement for Christianity. If Christianity has done that to him, then be not surprised that the world will not want it. But we hasten to say that Christianity has never produced despair or sourness in any life. A perverted notion of Christianity has produced it—but not true Christianity.

The sad, gloomy, dejected person is no shining light for Christianity. He advertises to the world that his religion—if he follows any—is too weak to sustain him in adverse circumstances. On the other hand, Christianity will support us—that is, if we support it.

• *Another inducement to a sunny disposition is that we may not be as bad off as we think*. You may have magnified your troubles. You may have let your imagination run wild. Your true condition may be much better than you have supposed. Think on the bright things in life. Be grateful for the good things you have. Your worrying over one thing you lack may have caused you to forget so many things you have. There is a lesson for us in the proverb: "I complained because I had no shoes until I saw a man who had no feet."

• *Another stimulant to high spirits is the indisputable fact that it pays.* Some virtues may delay their day of compensation, but cheerfulness pays now.

Cheerfulness pays by prolonging life. Doctors prescribe merriment for their patients. Solomon said, "A cheerful heart is good medicine, but a crushed spirit dries up the bones" (Proverbs 17:22). Science shows that our moods affect our health.

A bright outlook pays in that it minimizes our troubles. A sick man once said, "I have asthma, gout and six other maladies, but otherwise I am very well." Through his own outlook he lessened his burdens.

A sunny spirit will also pay us in friends. The cheerful person has a magnetism that pulls us to him. But the gloomy person repels us.

• *The promise that God will not leave us nor forsake us is another one of the many motives prompting good cheer.* God has said to His people, "Never will I leave you; never will I forsake you" (Hebrews 13:5). So take courage and be brave. When our human weaknesses seem so inadequate for life's problems and our heart is struck with fear, let us repeat this promise again and again.

When life gets as hard as it can get, God will be there. At night, He will lie beside you. In the morning, He

will be there. And in the day—
tomorrow and tomorrow and
tomorrow—He will walk by your side.

• *Hope is another powerful impulse to
cheerfulness.* Hope and gladness go
together. Solomon said, "The hope of
the righteous shall be gladness" (Proverbs 10:28).

Hope is the quality which makes life
worthwhile. It fills our untoward days
with happy anticipations. Civilization
rests on hope. The farmer plows in
hope. Last year the insects destroyed
his crops. The year before the floods
washed them away. And the year before that the drought stunted their
growth. But he plows and plants in
hope. He tells himself that it will be
better this year. Every business is
founded on hope. The merchant rents
a building, buys stock, and opens the
doors for business on hope. If all hope
were crushed, all humanity would die.
It is essential to life.

• *Another one of the many motives
prompting a sunshiny spirit is the
thought of eternal salvation.* Every
suffering, every disappointment, and
every sorrow seems so trivial and insignificant in comparison to the
thought of going home to heaven.
Hence, an apostle wrote, "For our
light and momentary troubles are
achieving for us an eternal glory, so
we fix our eyes not on what is seen,
but on what is unseen. For what is
seen is temporary, but what is unseen
is eternal" (II Corinthians 4:17, 18).

These afflictions are but for a moment,
comparatively speaking. By keeping
our eyes on heaven we get them off
our adversities. This is why they seem
but light afflictions for only a moment.
Despite the trials of the past and the
toils and disappointments of the
present, the anticipations of going
home puts a sparkle in our eyes, a
smile in our cheeks, and a song on

our lips. This earth is not our home.
Here we are just pilgrims passing
through. The thought of going home
is cheering.

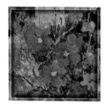

*To believe in heaven is not*

*to run away from life; it is to*

*run toward it.*

JOSEPH D. BLINCO

*Chapter Seven*

# INNER PEACE

Judy Buswell
©'99

*We are living in a complex age. Modern civilization is crowded with problems. But the greatest problem is man himself. All other problems are comparatively insignificant. The world's greatest fear is not the bomb, but he person who handles it. The power of atoms handled by a saint constitutes less of a threat to civilization than a small pistol handled by a criminal. Therefore, if we would help the world, we must help humanity; and if we would save the world, we must save humanity.*

• *Our greatest need in this warring world is not world peace but inner peace.* Peace of soul comes first. We struggle with others because first of all the struggle rages within ourselves. Cain had trouble with his brother Abel and slew him (Genesis 4:1-8),

because Cain first of all had trouble with himself—the trouble of envy and hatred. This first murderer's own inner conflict alienated him from his brother. Frustrated souls almost without an exception blame everybody but themselves for their troubles. They cannot have peace with others because they are not at peace with themselves. The battle in the field is the outgrowth of the battle in the heart.

The very nature of sin is such that it intensifies the sinner's opposition to the righteous. This happened to Cain. The cause of his frustration was within himself. The passing of the centuries has not changed humanity. The problems of the past will always be the problems of the present and of the future. We have new people, but the same old problems—external conflicts which are born of frustration within our hearts.

What can be done to take us off of

the treadmill of fears, nerves, and frustrations? How can we cure the frightening anxieties and find peace of soul? First, we must learn the cause of the frustration. If we cure the cause, the effect will take care of itself. Since we are no different from the people of the Bible, then we can go to the Bible and find both the cause and its cure.

• *The case of the Prodigal Son is enlightening* (Luke 15). He became alienated from himself, and this led him to withdraw from others and from God. His inner conflict had its beginning in his departing from himself. Not having any great objective in life, he heard the call of many voices. And he began to answer them, but none would satisfy. His life became locked in a prison of self, and this shut him off from others and from God. Estrangement from others and God are sure to result when we live only for ourselves and for this world. He asked

for his part of the estate. It was given to him. He left his father and family, friends and country. But neither life nor money was used for good. He wasted his days and his money in riotous living. It brought him low, to starvation, disgrace, and to a friendless state. In his blind and reckless search for inner peace he merely drove himself farther from it. Life became cruel to him because he was cruel to it.

After reaching the hog-pen level in life, "he came to himself." This is the key that unlocked the prison of his own making. He came back to his better self. He thought of home, his early training, helpful service to others, honest toil, clean relationships, and the days when his conscience was clear. Those were the good days. The only wise thing was to travel the hard road back to his former state. To refuse would have only aggravated his troubles. He had to go back or his condi-

tion would have worsened. So his way was clear. He said, "I will arise and go to my Father, and will say unto him, Father, I have sinned against heaven, before thy, and am no more worthy to be called thy son: make me as one of the hired servants."

The Prodigal's getting away from his better self had its roots in getting away from God. We were created in the spiritual image of God. We are spirit as well as flesh. Hence, living solely for the flesh will never satisfy our deeper longings. Some, not willing to return to the Father as did the Prodigal Son, have sought escape from their godlessness in violent hatred of God and severe persecution of religion. This, however, has never brought them peace—just more trouble.

Let us note what is implied in the young man's going back home. He came to himself—rational thinking. He went back to man from whom he had departed—sociable thinking. He went back to humility—claimed nothing special, no veneered righteousness. He went back to the fields of toil—honest labor. He went back to a busy and fruitful life— idleness was no fun. He went back to face the realities of life. He went back to God, for the father in the parable represents God. He went back to his true self.

What did he leave? He left egotism— his "ego" was not practical, just a false front that anyone could see through. He left idleness—it had only increased his miseries. He left a dream world—because life is real. He left a false view of the living—he learned that to eat, drink and be merry are not the true ends of living. He left behind his material conception of happiness—he acquired the much needed lesson that happiness comes from being neither rich nor poor, for he had vainly tried both. He left selfishness—from his grim experiences, he learned that the world did not revolve around himself. He left a life of sin—it had not satisfied. Summed up, he left behind a perverted self.

He came to himself. He went back home, and he found peace.

• *If we find peace, we must find it within ourselves.* The Prodigal Son found it right where he had left it— within himself. Every one who loses peace, does so through his own thinking. To regain peace, we must change our thinking and come to ourselves. This enables us to come back to God and to man. The thing the Prodigal wanted most was at first too close for him to see it. Oftentimes there is gold at our feet that we cannot see, because we look beyond it.

We knew a man who literally did this. He spent a lifetime looking for literal gold. With pick in his hand, he diligently sought the magic ore in the hills, breaks and streams in the Red River country. Finally he stumbled on what he thought to be the precious metal. His find was kept very secret. But the assayer said, "It is not gold; it is a metal called fool's gold." He first tried not to believe it, but there was no alternative. Facts are facts. He finally died a broken, disappointed, poverty-stricken old man. The irony of it is shortly after he died, a well was drilled on his little farm, and a new kind of gold—oil, flowing black gold—was found in abundant quantities. Gold was there at his feet, but he never found it because he never thought of looking for it at home.

While this was literally true of this one man, it is figuratively and spiritually true of millions of others. They seek this inner peace in every place except their inner self. The

paradoxical thing it that it is there in their own heart where they left it and can be found only by returning to it. Any outward peace they found is merely superficial.

• *The world is filled with lessons which teach us that peace does not depend upon outside circumstances.* This is seen in the works of two painters. Each painted a picture to portray his conception of true peace. The first chose for his painting a still, peaceful, lone lake high up in the mountains. The second painted on his canvas a roaring rushing waterfall, with an uncertain and fragile tree bending over the white foam. A robin sat on its nest at the fork of the branch.

The first was only stillness. The second was true peace—peace unrelated to outside circumstances. The little bird knew no anxiety. The twig on which he rested seemed unsafe to us. But there as he tossed and swayed in the wind, he joyously sang. He was indifferent to the water's spray and the twig's bend. For he had wings folded at his side. If he fell, he simply fell on his power to be lifted heavenward; for the sky was his home. This was peace which came from within.

> *Be like the bird, who*
> *Halting in his flight*
> *On limb too slight*
> *Feels it give way beneath him,*
> *Yet sings*
> *Knowing he hath wings*
>
> VICTOR HUGO

The life of Jesus was like that second painting. He was superior to all storms and trials because He had wings. No other man has had such serenity of soul, and no other man has had such a hectic stay in a restless world. Outwardly, Christ's life was filled with conflicts. Inwardly, there was peace as calm as a sea of glass. And even when His enemies were hounding Him for His life, He turned to troubled men, and as a last legacy offered them peace. He said, "Peace I leave with you, my peace I give you" (John 14:27).

*All of us desire peace, but very few desire those things that make for peace.*

THOMAS A' KEMPIS

*Chapter Eight*

# DISCOVERING INNER PEACE

*The world is filled with people who pace themselves like an imprisoned lion within his cage. They are seeking release from an unknown something, which is actually themselves. They imprisoned themselves through their own thoughts, attitudes, and ways of living.*

Now they seek escape. They want something more satisfying than food and freedom, strength and security. They want a food different from that the world lives on—they want food that feeds the soul. They long for a freedom that civilization as a whole does not know—freedom of mind. They want a new kind of strength and security, yet it is old—the strength and security which comes from within. They want to be something. They want something to live with, and something to live for. They want peace!

Their cries for help are heard all the world over. A thousand answers come back. But only a few offer anything worthwhile. Not finding the constructive answer, they often enslave themselves all the more to drink, gambling, lust, strife, hate, envy, jealousy, suspicion, and bitterness. They resent the world and complain about it. But if they will become different, they will find the world different. If we want peace, there are certain things we must do.

• *We must make up our minds to be happy.* What we decide will largely influence our state. For as a man, "thinketh in heart, so is he" (Proverbs 23:7 KJV). One can think himself into being miserable. A man once said, "When I feel good, I always feel bad; because I know that I am going to feel worse later." His thinking did this to him. The pessimist is always a creature of his own thinking.

Begin to cultivate peace within yourself now. It is not a luxury to be denied for sixty years because you are unable to afford it now. Habits grow, and one who says "tomorrow" will soon make tomorrow the rule of life. He who waits until tomorrow yields to a mischievous illusion. There is no such day as tomorrow; it is only a mirage, a fool's paradise. Yesterday is buried, tomorrow is unborn; therefore, today holds life and death, peace and conflict in its living hands. One of the great words in the Bible is "today."

• *We must learn that inner peace is mental rather than geographical.* "Oh! That I were somewhere else," is the attitude of malcontents. If they live in the country, they spend years trying to get to the city; if they get to the city, they spend the rest of their lives trying to save enough to get back to the country. Contentment does not depend upon where we are, but rather what we are. This is why a man of the Bible who has faced strong opposition much of his life could say, "I have learned to be content whatever the circumstances" (Philippians 4:11).

> *Fixed to no spot is happiness sincere*
> *'Tis nowhere to be found, or everywhere;*
> *'Tis never to be bought, but always free.*

POPE

• *We must be ourselves.* God made us different. No two people are exactly alike. Each must be himself in order to be happy. Certainly this does not bar self-improvement; but as one improves, he does it as himself. If you are yourself, then you will not have to worry about false pretenses. Contentment is derived from doing things your own way. Mass imitation or conformity is having a powerful impact on man's emotional well-being. It is developing within him hesitancy, tenseness, and insecurity. He is never sure of himself until he learns the wishes of others, to do right and trust in God. Then we can boldly say, "The Lord is my helper; I will not be afraid. What can man do to me?" (Hebrews 13:6).

• *We must accept ourselves as we are.* An acceptance of self is essential to contentment. We must accept the fact that different people have different talents and different degrees of ability (Matthew 25:14-30). We must reconcile ourselves to our own limitations.

Self-acceptance means that we shall not indulge in useless worry over what nature did not give us. Some things cannot be helped. For instance, Jesus said, "Which of you by taking thought can add one cubit unto his stature?" Worrying about our height will make us neither taller nor shorter. We are on the road to happiness if we accept ourselves as we are, even though we had severe handicaps. A woman once said that the happiest day of her life was the day she accepted the fact that she would never win a beauty contest.

In accepting self we should turn our obstacles into steppingstones. Fanny J. Crosby, the famous song writer, became blind at six weeks of age. In later years she testified: "I am the happiest soul living. If I had not been deprived of my sight, I would never have received so good an education, nor have been able to do good to so many people." This was so much better than despair which could have driven her to the streets to beg. Whatever our handicap is, accept it; conquer it; turn it into a victory. May we accept ourselves as we are and work from there.

• *We must make the least of what we*

*lack.* We do not need very much and do not need that little very long. A man of good circumstances once said, "I look at what I lack and count myself unhappy. Others look at what I have and count me happy." We have a great difficulty in defining "enough." After all, real riches are in the mind—in the mind's attitude. Contentment consists not in multiplying our wealth, but in decreasing our wants.

> *True happiness in to no place*
> *confined;*
> *But still is found in a contented*
> *mind.*

• *We must make the most of what we have.* Peace of mind comes from using what we possess. The five-talent man could say, "Master you have entrusted me with five talents: See, I have gained five more" (Matthew 25:20). This accomplishment was a matter of great satisfaction to him. Neither riches nor poverty has the inherent power to make any mortal happy. Instead, happiness comes from making the most of what we have, whether little or much. While it is evident that wealth is a very convenient thing, it is also admitted that the poor man who enjoys his little is much richer than the wealthy man who gets no joy from his plenty. So the only standard by which we can conclude when we are really rich is peace of mind.

• *We must live so that our conscience will approve.* Many frustrated lives have their roots in a condemning conscience. Since man must live with himself, then he ought to keep himself fit to live with. "Dear friends, if our hearts do not condemn us, we have confidence before God"(I John 3:21).

• *We must be unselfish.* Through selfishness we destroy ourselves. It reminds us of the two goats which met on a narrow bridge high over a river.

Neither would give way to the other. The result: selfishness destroyed them both. Selfishness destroys character, shrinks the soul, and makes us miserable. The one who seeks joy for self only, loses it. On the other hand, he who drives away the clouds for others will make some sunshine for himself. "Each of you should look not only to your own interests, but also to the interests of others" (Philippians 2:4) is the happiest way to live.

• *We must stay busy in profitable works.* Idleness is an enemy of contentment. The most miserable people in the world are those who have nothing to do but have a good time. Our take-it-easy complex has led to more licentious living, wickedness, and crime. A nation that had a philosophy of work did not have so much restlessness and discontent; neither was it plagued with so many ulcers and nervous breakdowns; nor were there so many skid rows and jails.

God's law of work is essential to our happiness (II Thessalonians 3:11, 12).

> *Make use of time, let not*
> *advantage slip;*
> *Beauty within itself should not*
> *be wasted;*
> *Fair flowers, that are not gath'rd*
> *in their prime*
> *Rot and consume themselves in*
> *little time.*

SHAKESPEARE

• *We must let go of the past.* "Forgetting what is behind," is a necessary principle of happy living (Philippians 3:13). One of the greatest of arts is the art of forgetting. If we have made mistakes, derive what wisdom we can from them and forget them. If we have sinned, comply with God's law of pardon so that we may receive forgiveness. Then forget it. When God forgives sin He remembers it no more. We should forget it too! Almost every life has its own closet of skeletons. We should not try to resurrect them. They belong to the never-changing past. What counts is what we do with today.

> *Life, like war, is a series of mistakes; and he is not the best Christian nor the best general who makes the fewest false steps. He is the best who wins the most splendid victories by the retrieval of mistakes.*
>
> F. W. ROBERTSON

• *We must maintain a noble relationship with God.* This sums it up, for it is our whole duty (Ecclesiastes 12:13). This is the one duty out of which all other duties grow. He who keeps it keeps himself and in so doing finds inner peace. But "the way of transgressor is hard." Sin is the most deceitful master with which we must deal. It offers joy but gives sorrow; holds out peace but gives frustration.

As we have seen, inner peace is a by-product of so many other things. We cannot pursue it directly. When we live as God would have us, His peace will come.

# Chapter Nine

# BE OF GOOD COURAGE

*This* was God's message to Joshua. Heavy responsibilities weighed upon Joshua, enough to frighten any man. The job cut out for him demanded heroism. He needed courage. So God spoke these assuring words, "Be strong and courageous. Do not be terrified; do not be discouraged, for the Lord your God will be with you wherever you go" (Joshua 1:9).

• *Courage is one of our direst needs,* because fear is one of our deadliest foes. Courage is a basic trait of a strong character. Physical courage enables a person to triumph over the fear of risking life for a person or cause. Moral courage gives us power to stand against society's criticism, ridicule, and persecution. Another type of courage is just plain old everyday courage which leads us to be brave amid all the wear and strain, friction and opposition of life. He who fights well his own battle of life is no less the hero than a person who fights in national armies. Heroism is where you find it, and not necessarily behind a gun. The daily circumstances of some people demand a type of courage unexcelled. They have brave hearts or they would give up the fight. The discouraged man simply lacks courage; and he becomes anxious and fearful. This disqualifies him for his best work.

• *Fear is a paralyzing thing.* We may be struck by many storms which do not wreck us, but the storm of fear hits hard and plays havoc with us. It makes the hands unsteady, the knees tremble, and the heart weak. It has blighted many fond hopes and killed many worthy endeavors. It has blocked spiritual, social, and business progress. Many persons with considerable ability and many other admirable qualities have failed because they lacked this one necessary trait to succeed—courage.

• *The cause of our fears is usually imaginary instead of real.* Oftentimes we are frightened by false alarms. The past teaches us that most things we feared were only the creations of our own fearful mind. We have scared ourselves! We have been afraid of the darkness when in reality the sun was shining. The thing we feared was only a passing shadow from a fast-moving cloud.

> *Though life is made up of mere bubbles*
>
> *'Tis better than many aver,*
> *For while we've a whole lot of troubles*
> *The most of them never occur.*
>
> NIXON WATERMANN

• *Whatever our state is, life should be lived realistically and courageously.* Even real problems are not too hard, if we have the courage to face them. Perhaps you have seen a child with a cut finger, holding it off at a distance with head turned, afraid to look at it. But when he got the courage to face his little difficulty and permit treatment, then it was not so terrible. Maybe this is one reason we grow less afraid as we grow older—at least, those of us who have borne many sorrows and faced many trials . We have found all of our problems solved, one way or another, when we looked them straight in the face and came to grips with them.

• *Both courage and fear are affairs of the heart.* Each is an inward condition that controls outward behavior in times of trial, peril, and difficulty. So if we would cure ourselves of fear, we must look within ourselves. Outside forces may give us temporary relief, but definitely no cure. Fear is produced by a cause; and when that cause is removed, courage will fill the heart instead. Here are some causes of fear:

1) With some, fear is the by-product of selfishness. Self-interest may cause a person to be so concerned with what is affecting him that fear grips and controls him. Fear increases with our self-regard. An inflated balloon is more vulnerable than one not blown up. Likewise, the more one becomes blown up with self-love the larger target he becomes for fear to hit him. Self-centeredness with all its idle preoccupation is a fountainhead of fear. To overcome, it we must find some interest which is so great and worthwhile that it causes us to lose ourselves in the bigger issue.

2) Fear also springs from doubt. Doubt has fear; faith has courage. Someone wrote, "Fear knocked at the door. Faith opened it. No one was there." Faith drives away fear. Blessed is the person who believes in God, himself, and others. Many people are shot through and through with an inferiority complex which stems from their little faith in themselves. They believe their doubts and doubt their beliefs. They doubt that they can measure up to what society demands of them. Quit doubting yourself. Just trust in the Lord and do the best you can—and let the results take care of themselves. No person succeeds at everything all the time—from business proposals to chocolate pies—and the world does not expect it.

The best way to believe in self is first to believe in God. As faith in God increases, faith in self also increases, and as faith increases, fear decreases. One of the world's greatest leaders overcame fear through faith. This was

Moses. The Bible says, "By faith he forsook Egypt, not fearing the wrath of the king."

3) "Conscience makes cowards of us all." An accusing conscience runs wild with imagination. As an extreme example, it is said that Bessus, a Grecian, pulled down the bird's nests about his house because he stated that the birds never ceased to accuse him of the murder of his father. The singing of the little birds were songs of peace; but to this fearful man with a gnawing conscience they were sounds of condemnation.

> *It is the nature and quality of a guilty conscience to flee and be terrified, even when all is well, and prosperity abounds, and to change such prosperity into danger.*
>
> MARTIN LUTHER

Keep your conscience clear, and it will be a source of courage.

4) Fear also arises from a sense of loneliness. The solitary soul is more easily scared. The presence of others gives us courage. A soldier may be afraid to make a dangerous mission alone, but fights bravely with mates at his side. The thought of dying alone terrifies him, but he can make the supreme sacrifice in the presence of others without a whimper of fear.

No one is alone when God is with him. The presence and companionship of God drives away fear. A little child is afraid in the dark, but only when the mother is away. When the mother's hand is laid on the child's cheek, courage enters that little one's heart. God's presence in life is a safeguard against fear, an assurance against evil, and an inspiration to courage.

The Bible says: "So do not fear, for I am with you; do not be dismayed, for I am your God. I will strengthen you

CHAPTER NINE

and help you" (Isaiah 41:10). The same God who spoke these words to Israel still lives. We are not afraid, because he marches by our side.

*Courage, brother! do not*
*stumble,*
*Though thy path be dark*
*as night;*
*There's a star to guide the*
*humble;*
*Trust in God and do*
*the Right.*

MACLEOD

# Chapter Ten

# I WILL FEAR NO EVIL

*It* was David the shepherd poet who said, "I will fear no evil" (*Psalm 23:4*). While these words were spoken by David, they are meant to be an inspiration to all of us. "I will fear no evil"—no past, nor present or future evil; no imaginary or real evil; "for thou art with me."

But we unnecessarily keep on being scared. Here are some common fears:

• *Some fear sickness.* But fearing it is the best way to develop it. Do not fear sickness; the ailment you fear may never come. If it does come, it may be a blessing in disguise.

Both the well and the sick have reason to hope for a longer life. Every day we learn more about the things given by the gracious God to cure us of our ailments. And every day we learn more about how to preserve health. Conse-

quently, the span of life is being lengthened.

We fear what we think may interfere with our progress and happiness. Sickness does not necessarily have to hinder either. Some of the happiest people we know have been afflicted with ill health for many years. Some of the world's most successful people worked their way up in spite of physical handicaps. This was true of Robert Louis Stevenson. He never saw a well day in his life. But he left to the world a great legacy of literature. Examples could be multiplied. Strength of will lifted them above their afflictions. They did not give up! Neither were they afraid!

After all, the best health is the ability to live in bad health undaunted and unafraid.

Our greatest problem is not how to add years to life, but how to add life to years. This way we can live while we live. To do this, we must not be afraid!

• *Some fear that they may not have enough material things in life.* These fearful people need to realize that we can eat only one meal at a time, wear only one suit at a time, and occupy only one room at a time. Really, we do not need very much. We forget that life is more than meat and the body is more than raiment. Christ pointed to the birds and said to a people who felt their insecurity, "Your heavenly Father feeds them. Are you not worth more than they?" If a sparrow cannot fly throughout the heavens without attracting His attention, surely the needs of His people cannot go unnoticed.

## The Sparrow

*I am only a little sparrow,*
*A bird of low degree;*

*My life is of little value,*
*But the dear Lord cares for me.*

*If my meal is sometimes scanty,*
*Close picking makes it sweet;*
*I have always enough to feed me,*
*And "life is more than meat."*

*Though small, we are not*
*forgotten;*
*Though weak we are never afraid;*
*For we know that the dear Lord*
*keepeth*
*The life of the creatures he made.*

God has given us brain and brawn, summer and winter, sunshine and rain, sprouting and harvest. His blessings are too numerous to count. And in our affluent society, most of us do not have to fear starvation. We have to decide when *enough* is *enough* and stop trying to endlessly accumulate things.

*Others fear failure in life.* But what is success? This depends entirely upon the gauges we use. All God expects is that we do our best. He who does much—comparatively speaking—with little has succeeded, while he who has done little—comparatively speaking—with much has failed. It is not how much we do, but how much we do with what we have that spells success. The person who does his best should never fear failure, for he is a success.

> *The world is wide*
> *In time and tide*
> *And God is guide;*
> *Then do not hurry.*
> *That man is blest*
> *Who does his best*
> *And leaves the rest;*
> *Then do not worry*
>
> CHARLES F. DEEMS

Success cannot be measured in terms of a few "flash-in-the-pan" achievements. True success is to fear God and keep His commandments (Ecclesiates 12:1). Hence, success cannot be fully determined until the end of life.

> *Let no one till his death*
> *Be called unhappy. Measure*
> *not the work*
> *Until the day's out and the*
> *labor done;*
> *Then bring your gauges.*
>
> ELIZABETH BARRETT BROWNING

*Others fear society.* They fear what others may think, feel, and say. They live in fear that their dress, automobile, home, furniture, speech, and job may not be good enough to please the critical and heartless world. This is truly a foolish fear. What difference does it make how others feel, if we do not hurt them! They are not our standard. They have no right to run our lives. They have all they can do to run their own. Futhermore, it is futile to try to please everybody. No one can do it. No even Jesus Christ could. So there is but one intelligent thing to do; please God, live your own life, run your own business, and let others think what they will. You will be surprised by how much better you will feel and how much more you will be appreciated. There is entirely too much tendency to put everybody in the same mold of public opinion. Be yourself!

If you are having trouble overcoming this fear, then learn well these verses from the Bible and quote them often:

> The Lord is my helper; I will not
> be afraid. What can man do to me?
> HEBREWS 13:6

> The Lord is with me; I will not be
> afraid. What can man do to me?
> PSALM 118:6

• *Some fear old age.* How useless! For no one has the power to hold back the hands of the clock of life. Whether we like it or not, they just keep on turning at the same speed. Regardless of age, life is still what we make it. There is nothing to fear in old age when we realize that our accomplishments and abilities need not necessarily decline with the accumulation of years. There is a world of evidence to teach us this is right. For instance: Commodore Vanderbilt between 70 and 83 added about 100 million to his fortune. Verdi at 74 produced his masterpeice , "Othello;" at 80 "Falstaff," and at 85, the famous "Ave Maria." Cato at 80 began the study of Greek. When asked why he began the study of such a difficult language so late in life, he replied, "Because I didn't start sooner." Tennyson at 83 wrote "Crossing the Bar."

It is never too late! Old age can be the happiest and most fruitful years

of life. By virtue of experience, the aged should be able to give more to life and thus get more from it. Age is grossly misunderstood! These poetic words shed light on what it actually is:

*An age so blest that, by its side Youth seems the wasted instead.*

ROBERT BROWNING

Even though we are old in years we can still be young in heart. There is nothing to fear in age. We can so live that our last years will be our best. Praying the beautiful thoughts written by John Greenleaf Whittier will enrich our riper years.

*Fill, brief or long, my granted years*
*Of life with love to thee and man;*
*Strike when thou wilt, the hour of rest,*
*But let my last days be my best.*

• *Many fear death.* Death was designed, however, as one of our most needed blessings. The Bible says, "Precious in the sight of Jehovah is the death of his saints." It was not good for man to live forever in a world of sin, rebellion, and strife. So God arranged for the dissolution of flesh and spirit which is called death. God intended for death to serve as an exit to this world and an entrance to another world.

In God's plan of this things, death is necessary because "flesh and blood cannot inherit the kingdom of God." These bodies of flesh and blood are not suited to an eternal habitation. We have to lay them aside that our souls may be clothed with new bodies "like unto His glorious body."

In this present world, we must have death in order to have life. Suppose no one should ever die—many births but no deaths—life would soon become unbearable. Think how terrible it would be if suffering people could not die.

Death was designed to be gain. The Bible says, "To live is Christ and to die is gain." This solves the problem of life, and then there is no problem to death. Take care of life, and death will take care of itself. Then you can say in the comforting language of David in the Twenty-Third Psalm: "Yea, though I walk through the valley of the shadow of death, I will fear no evil: for thou art with me." There is courage to be gained in repeating again and again this verse from the Bible. Make it one of your rules of life.

*So live that when thy summons comes to join*
*The innumerable caravan which moves*
*To that mysterious realm where each shall take*
*His chamber in the silent halls of death,*
*Thou go not like the quarry slave at night*
*Scourged to his dungeon ; but, sustained and soothed*
*By an unfaltering trust, approach thy grave*
*Like one who wraps the drapery of his couch*
*About him and lies down to pleasant dreams.*

THANATOPSIS, WILLIAM CULLEN BRYANT

The phrase "fear not" occurs eighty-one times in the Bible. God meant for His people to be unafraid. We would expect that of Him since He knows no fears. It is His will that we do our best in life, and this is impossible if we are fearful. There is nothing to fear but God, and that fear is different, a fear joined with love and hope like a son a respects his father. It can be summed up in one statement: the person who fears God has no cause for any other fear.

*The remarkable thing about fearing God is that when you fear God, you fear nothing else. But if you do not fear God, you fear everything else.*

OSWALD CHAMBERS